DATE DUE

GAYLORD			PRINTED IN U.S.A.

GIRLS' GUIDES

Fuel Up!

A Girl's Guide to Eating Well

● **Leslie Levchuck, RD** ●

the rosen publishing group's
rosen central
new york

To my family, for giving me the fuel.

Published in 1999 by The Rosen Publishing Group, Inc.
29 East 21st Street, New York, NY 10010

First Edition

Library of Congress Cataloging-in-Publication Data

Levchuck, Leslie.
    Fuel up! : a girl's guide to eating well / by Leslie Levchuck. —
1st ed.
        p.   cm.
    Includes bibliographical references and index.
    ISBN 0-8239-2981-7 (lib. bdg.)
    1. Children—Nutrition.   I. Title.
TX361.C5L48   1999
613.2'083—dc21
                                            99-17213
                                                CIP

Manufactured in the United States of America

nts

About This Book

The middle school years are like a roller coaster—wild and scary but also fun and way cool. One minute you're way, way up there, and the next minute you're plunging down into the depths. Not surprisingly, sometimes you may find yourself feeling confused and lost. Not to worry, though. Just like on a roller-coaster ride, at the end of all this crazy middle school stuff, you'll be laughing and screaming and talking about how awesome it all was.

Right now, however, chances are your body is changing so much that it's barely recognizable, your old friends may not share your interests anymore, and your life at school is suddenly hugely complicated. And let's not even get into the whole boy issue. It's a wonder that you can still think straight at all.

Fortunately, reader dear, help is here. This book is your road map. It's also a treasure chest filled with ideas and advice. Armed with this book and with your own inner strength (trust us, you have plenty), you can safely, confidently navigate the twists and turns of your middle school years. It will be tough going, and sometimes you'll wonder if you'll ever get through it. But you—fabulous, powerful, unique you—are up to the task. This book is just a place to start.

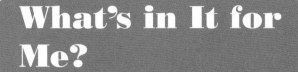

What's in It for Me?

Food. You eat it when you're hungry; you love it when it tastes good. What else is there to say about it? Well, if you want a healthy, happy bod, there are a few details that you should know:

Eating well and staying fit give you the power to help you perform your best.

There is no such thing as a good food or a bad food—just a good or bad diet.

Weight loss and dieting can prevent you from growing to your full height and can keep your bones from developing properly.

Girls who eat breakfast learn better, are more alert, and have more energy than those who skip the morning meal.

As many as 86 percent of teenage girls are not getting the calcium their bodies need every day.

Your body loses iron each time you have your period, and if you don't replace it by eating iron-rich foods, you may feel weak and tired.

Some fast-food salads are so crammed with fatty extras and gloppy dressing that they have more fat and calories than a deluxe burger.

Regular exercise not only builds stronger bones and muscles; it also builds confidence, improves self-esteem, and can relieve stress.

You Are What You Eat

Did you ever hear the expression "You are what you eat"? Do you know that the food choices you make today will affect the way you look, feel, and perform tomorrow? Believe it! The food you eat affects your weight, your height, your skin, your smile, your eyes, and many other parts of you.

Your body needs more than forty different nutrients every day. Nutrients are substances found in food that have specific roles in keeping your body going. The nutrients we get from food are vitamins, minerals, carbohydrates, fats, proteins, and water. To understand how important each nutrient is to proper health, think of your body as a car that needs gas. The food you eat provides the "gas," or energy, to keep you going. Calories (the units of energy in food) come from essential nutrients called carbohydrates, fats, and proteins. But just as a car needs more than gas to keep going (like spark plugs and oil, for example), your body needs many other nutrients in order to run smoothly. Vitamins, minerals, and water are also essential nutrients, though they do not provide calories.

Every day, your body depends on you to make good food choices so that it gets all of these nutrients in the right amounts. There is no one food that can provide everything you need. Eating a variety of foods every day and balancing it with regular physical activity is what will help you look, feel, and be your best.

Back to the Future

As a teenager, you're probably not too concerned about how you are going to look and feel when you are your mother's or grandmother's age. But chances are you do care about looking good, maintaining a healthy weight, and having lots of energy right now.

Surprise: Choosing healthy eating habits will help you with all of these things! Take care of your "insides" by eating the foods your body needs, and you'll notice a difference in your "outsides" as well.

Think of it as living from the inside out. Not only will you feel better and have more energy when you eat well, but your skin, teeth, and hair will also reflect your good choices. Making the right choices now will help you to look and feel your best today and help prevent serious health problems like heart disease, cancer, and stroke later in life.

You eat food for energy, in order to be active, and let's face it, because it tastes good! Eating well does not mean eating food you don't like "because it's good for you." All foods—even cheeseburgers and ice cream—can be part of a healthy diet, depending on how much you have and how often you eat them. It's important that these foods fit into your eating plan and don't crowd out more nutritious foods. In order to get all of the nutrients your body needs every day and avoid overeating, you have to think before you eat. The food pyramid can help you make the right choices. Sound complicated? Too much to bother with? Read on to see how easy it is to fit healthy eating habits into your busy, active life.

Ms. Quiz: Rate Your Plate

How do you know if your eating habits need improvement or not? To see where you stand, take this quickie quiz about your usual eating and exercise habits.

1. How often do you eat candy or chocolate?
a) less than once a day   b) once a day   c) more than once a day   d) every chance I get!

2. How many cans of soda or bottles of sweetened fruit juice do you drink?
a) less than one a day   b) one a day   c) two or three a day   d) I swig soda or juice all day long

3. How many servings of dairy foods (milk, yogurt, or cheese) do you have on a typical day?
a) at least two servings   b) one serving   c) zero, zilch, zip

4. How much physical activity do you get in an average week?
a) at least thirty minutes, three times a week
b) less than thirty minutes, three times a week
c) less than thirty minutes, once a week   d) Does getting out of bed count as physical activity?

5. How many servings of fruits and vegetables do you eat per day?
a) five or more   b) two or three   c) one, on a good day   d) What are fruits and vegetables?

6. When you eat a meal, you
a) stop eating before you feel full   b) eat until it hurts   c) leave nothing on your plate besides the pattern

7. When you drink milk, you usually choose
a) low-fat or nonfat (skim) milk   b) whole milk   c) no milk

8. Do you eat breakfast, lunch, and dinner on most days?
a) yes   b) no, just lunch and dinner   c) no, just dinner

If you answered mostly (a), you're practically a pro at fueling up for good health! If your answers were mostly (b), your eating habits need some work. If you answered mostly (c) or (d), you could definitely use a nutrition refresher course—that is, if you feel healthy enough to get out of bed!

How Does Your Pyramid Stack Up?

The Wonders of the Food Pyramid

You've almost certainly seen the food pyramid somewhere—on a cereal box, in the grocery store, or maybe in health class. You may be wondering what ever happened to the four basic food groups we used to hear about. You might also want to know why this food guide is shaped like a pyramid. What's it supposed to tell us, anyway?

The food pyramid was developed by the U.S. Department of Agriculture (USDA) as a guide to help you choose a healthy diet that is right for you. Its shape is important to its message. Like the great pyramids of Egypt, the food pyramid is built on a strong foundation and gets its strength from the many different-size blocks that fit together to make a solid structure. (The food pyramid's blocks are made up of food groups rather than rocks, so it's a tastier pyramid than the ones in Egypt.)

These are the key points of the food pyramid:

> *Eat a variety of foods every day.*
> *Choose foods with less fat and sugar.*
> *Eat plenty of whole-grain foods, fruits, and vegetables.*

"Variety" means eating different foods among and within the different food groups. Remember—no one food has everything your body needs, so you should eat a variety of foods every day.

For cultural or religious reasons, or because of personal beliefs or preferences, you may find that the food pyramid is not the best guide for you. Other food pyramids have been developed for vegetarians (people who don't eat meat) and for people of various different cultural backgrounds. The individual food groups in these pyramids differ somewhat, but each pyramid stresses the importance of variety, balance, and healthy choices. The next sections describe the food categories used in the USDA food pyramid.

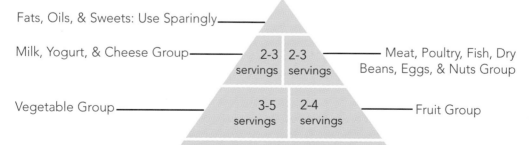

Fats, Oils, & Sweets: Use Sparingly

Milk, Yogurt, & Cheese Group — 2-3 servings

2-3 servings — Meat, Poultry, Fish, Dry Beans, Eggs, & Nuts Group

Vegetable Group — 3-5 servings

2-4 servings — Fruit Group

6-11 servings
Bread, Cereal, Rice, and Pasta Group

13

Bread, Cereal, Rice, and Pasta Group

A healthy diet begins with plenty of foods from the bread, cereal, rice, and pasta group (also called the grain group). This food category has a very important position in the pyramid—the foundation. Is this because it is the most important group? No! All groups are equally important. But you need more servings from the grain group than from any other category. Grain group foods provide complex carbohydrates and fiber to the body.

Complex carbohydrates come mainly from plant foods such as wheat, oats, and rice. Complex carbohydrates supply your body with a great source of energy. Your body doesn't use them up as quickly as it does simple carbohydrates, which come mainly from sugary foods.

Fiber helps push food through your digestive tract to get rid of wastes. It keeps your intestines in good working order. Not getting enough fiber can seriously mess up your digestion. Not all grain foods are high in fiber, though, and it's important to choose the right ones. Grains high in fiber include whole-wheat bread and crackers, brown rice, pasta, and whole-grain cereals (like Cheerios, raisin bran, and shredded wheat).

To get all of the complex carbohydrates and fiber your body needs, choose grain foods like bread, cereal, air-popped popcorn, pretzels, flour tortillas, rice, noodles, and crackers. Most foods in the grain group are low in fat, with a few exceptions. Doughnuts, pastries, muffins, and some crackers (especially butter- or cheese-flavored) can be high in fat, and—you guessed it—you should choose these foods less often.

> **Foolish Food Myth:** Grain group foods like pasta, rice, and bread are fattening.
>
> **Fascinating Food Fact:** No single food is "fattening"—some foods just provide more energy than others. It is your overall diet and the amount of exercise you get that are mainly responsible for increases or decreases in your weight.

Vegetable Group and Fruit Group

Working from the bottom up brings us to the next level of the food pyramid, where the vegetable and fruit groups are located. Fruits and vegetables are packed with vitamins and minerals and are naturally low in fat. Two vitamins that fruits and vegetables provide are especially important for your growing bod: vitamins A and C.

Vitamin A
Why You Need It:
It's important for night vision and healthy skin, gums, and teeth
Where You Can Get It:
carrots
sweet potatoes
spinach
grapefruit
cantaloupe
nectarines

Vitamin C
Why You Need It:
It's important for healthy gums and teeth, healing cuts and scrapes,
and bones
Where You Can Get It:
broccoli
green peppers
100 percent orange juice
pineapple
peaches
tomatoes

Fascinating Food Fact: Bananas are the most popular fruit in the United States.

Most people in the United States don't eat nearly enough servings of fruits and vegetables every day. Eating five or more servings may sound like a lot of work, but you can deal—and there are so many yummy choices! In fact, any fruit or vegetable is a good choice. Juice is fine too. Just remember to look for the words "100 percent fruit juice" on the label to be sure that you are getting all of the benefits of a fruit serving. It's also best to make sure that your juice doesn't have sugar added to it—pure fruit juice is sweet by itself, and the extra calories that added sugar provides are unnecessary. Eating a variety of fruits and vegetables every day is important since they don't all provide the same vitamins and minerals in the same amounts. Try to mix it up—don't eat the same fruits and vegetables all the time. (That would be totally boring anyway.) And don't always rely on fruit juice as your daily fruit serving—the whole fruit that the juice was made from contains fiber and will help fill you up.

Milk and Milk Products Group

The milk and milk products group includes milk, yogurt, and cheese. The key nutrient supplied by this group is calcium. Calcium is important for building strong bones and teeth and helping nerves and muscles function. Most Americans need a lot more calcium than they get.

There are four basic types of milk, which differ only in the amount of fat they contain. In spite of the difference in fat, all provide the same amount of calcium and other nutrients.

Who should be drinking which kind of milk? Well, to build strong bones without getting too much fat or calories, anyone older than two should be drinking low-fat milk—so if you're reading this book, that means you. One cup of whole milk has eight grams of fat. That's the same amount as three strips of bacon! Who needs all that fat? Only babies do. So which milk should you be drinking? Low-fat (1 percent) or non-fat (skim) milk will provide all the nutrients your body craves without the extra fat and calories. If you find regular nonfat milk too thin, try one of the extrarich varieties that you can find in most stores. Think of low-fat and nonfat milk as the food version of a super bargain at your favorite store— you get all that great calcium without having to "pay" for extra fat and calories. How can you say no to a deal like that?

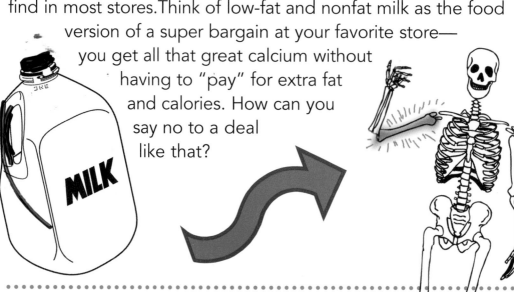

Growing girls need at least three servings from this group each day to get the calcium their bodies need to build strong bones.

NEWS FLASH: Beware! Some of the ready-made pudding cups available in grocery stores contain little or no calcium. Pudding made at home from milk is a much better source of calcium.

Even if you don't want to drink a glass of plain milk, it's easy to get three servings a day: Have low-fat milk on cereal in the morning, cheese on a sandwich at lunch, and low-fat yogurt or low-fat frozen yogurt for a snack. Choose part-skim or low-fat cheeses when available, and make your sweet tooth happy with desserts such as ice milk or low-fat frozen yogurt. You can also snack on pudding made from low-fat milk.

Meat and Meat Alternatives Group

The meat and meat alternatives group is the last major food category. This group provides the essential nutrients protein and iron. Protein is needed for maintaining your muscles, and iron is necessary for healthy blood. Don't be misled by the name of this food group, however. It includes not only red meat like hamburger and steak, but also chicken, turkey, fish, and seafood as well as eggs, peanut butter, nuts, and beans. Why? The latter foods are considered alternatives to or substitutes for meat because they are good sources of protein and iron.

What if you're a vegetarian? People choose a vegetarian diet for various reasons, including religion, culture, love and concern for animals, or just because they think meat is icky. Whatever the reason, non-meat-eaters can look to foods such as nuts, seeds, beans, peanut butter, tofu, and eggs and fish (if they eat them) as protein sources in their diet. A vegetarian diet can be healthy if it is planned carefully to make sure you are not missing important nutrients. If you are a vegan and eat no animal products at all, you will have to be extracareful about what you eat in order to stay healthy.

In general, most people in the United States get all the protein they need and usually more. If you have a sandwich at lunch that includes tuna, turkey, or chicken and another serving from the meat and meat alternatives group at dinner, you'll easily get your two recommended servings a day.

Some high-protein foods contain much more fat than others, and you should eat them less often. Those foods include bologna, salami, hot dogs, regular ground beef, fried chicken, and sausage. If you crave meat frequently, choose lean beef or pork and skinless chicken or turkey because these are lowest in fat. Fish is a good low-fat choice too, though some kinds of fish are higher in fat than others. Vegetarians can try low-fat tofu, beans, and low-fat meat substitutes. (Check the health food store or a large grocery store for these.)

Fats, Oils, and Sweets

The small tip of the pyramid contains fats, oils, and sweets. This trio is not considered a major food group. These foods provide fat, sugar, and calories with few nutrients. They should be enjoyed as occasional treats, not in place of foods in the other groups. (And in case you were wondering, the answer is no: The protein from the peanuts in your favorite candy bar doesn't make it a healthy food!)

The foods found in this group include salad dressing, butter, margarine, soda, candy, chips, and sweet desserts. Sure, that stuff tastes great, but you wouldn't want it to make up most of your diet. You wouldn't have much energy, and you would look and feel unhealthy. No recommended number of servings is given for this group because it's better to think of these foods as occasional extras rather than everyday fuel.

What's a Serving?

The following chart shows what counts as one serving from each of the five major food groups. If you eat more than the amount listed, count it as more than one serving. For example, if you eat a large plate of spaghetti, it would count as two or three servings from the grain group or maybe even more, depending on just how big that plate is.

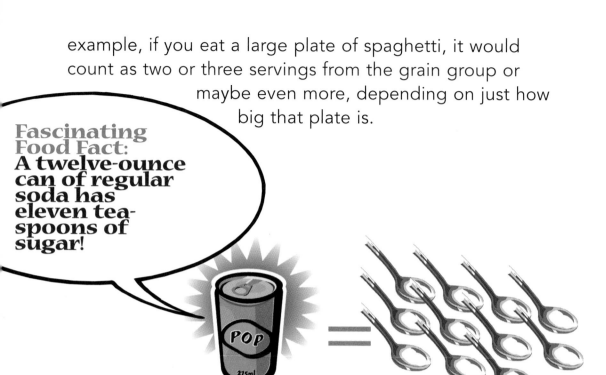

Fascinating Food Fact: A twelve-ounce can of regular soda has eleven teaspoons of sugar!

One Serving Equals:

Grain Group
1 slice of bread
1/2 hamburger or hot dog bun
1 ounce of cold cereal
1/2 cup of pasta, rice, or hot cereal
3-4 saltine-type crackers

Vegetable Group
1/2 cup of cooked or chopped raw vegetables
1 cup of lettuce or salad greens
3/4 cup of vegetable juice
10 french fries

Fruit Group
1 medium piece of fruit or melon wedge
3/4 cup of 100% fruit juice
1/2 cup of chopped, cooked, or canned fruit

Milk Group
1 cup of milk or yogurt (Make it low-fat!)
1 cup of frozen yogurt
1 1/2 ounces of natural cheese (cheddar, Swiss, etc.)
2 ounces of processed cheese

Meat Group
3 ounces of cooked meat or poultry
1/2 cup of cooked beans
1 egg
2 tablespoons of peanut butter

Diet and Disease

We've already mentioned that the way you eat can affect your health later in life. Eating well can help prevent major health problems like heart disease, stroke, diabetes, and cancer. There are also many other problems that can be prevented by making the right food choices now. Two health issues of special concern to girls and women are osteoporosis and anemia. These are conditions that can be caused by not getting enough of an essential mineral, and both are more common among girls and women than boys or men. (Lucky us.) So help yourself to more calcium and iron.

Bone Up on Calcium

Few girls get the amount of calcium their bodies need every day. As a matter of fact, eight out of every ten girls don't make the grade when it comes to calcium! Calcium is a mineral that is important for building bones, nerve impulses, blood clotting, and muscle contractions. During your teen years, you're growing taller, and your bone development shifts into high gear. You actually need more calcium now than when you were in grade school.

Believe it or not, your bones are growing right along with you. Nearly half of all the bone mass in your body is formed during your teenage years. The human skeleton is made up of 206 bones, all of which need a daily dose of calcium. When you eat calcium-rich foods, your body deposits some of this mineral in your bones, just as you might deposit money in the bank. If you don't get enough calcium from the foods you eat, it is gradually taken out of your bones. If you don't keep adding to your calcium "bank account" during your preteen and teen years, your bones won't develop the way they should. It's almost impossible to get enough calcium when you're older to make up for what you missed. In the short term, that means you might not be as tall or strong as you are meant to be. In the long term, it means that bones will be less dense (like Swiss cheese) and less able to withstand the natural loss that comes with aging.

Stat Chat

Twenty-five million Americans have osteoporosis, and four out of every five are women!

When too much bone mass is lost, bones can become brittle and weak and more likely to fracture or break. This condition is referred to as osteoporosis, or porous (full of holes and spaces) bones. If you make sure to get all the calcium you need now, you'll not only be healthier as a teen, but you'll also be way less likely to develop osteoporosis later in life.

So why are most girls flunking Basic Calcium? In part, the problem is due to poor eating habits, skipping meals, and dieting. You'll remember from chapter two that calcium is the key nutrient in the milk and dairy food group. And to get your body's daily requirement of this nutrient, you need to have three to four servings from that group. Milk and dairy foods provide the richest—and easiest—supply of calcium, but girls often drink less milk and more soda and sweetened drinks as they get older. Other items in the food pyramid besides milk and dairy products also provide calcium—but not as much. For example, you would have to eat a mega-quantity of broccoli—about four cups—to get the same amount of calcium that is in one cup of low-fat milk! So what's a girl to do if she doesn't like to drink milk? Try flavored milk (like chocolate or strawberry), have cereal with milk in the morning, have low-fat cheese on sandwiches at lunch, try fruit yogurt as a snack, and look for special varieties of bread and orange juice that are calcium-enriched.

Some girls may not be able to drink milk because it makes them feel bloated and gassy or even causes them to have diarrhea. These girls may have a condition called lactose intolerance. Lactose intolerance occurs when your body doesn't properly digest lactose, the natural sugar in milk. As a result, your body produces excessive gas. Fortunately, people with this condition can buy lactose-reduced milk in most grocery stores. If you're lactose intolerant, other dairy foods may not give you these symptoms, so be sure to include them in your diet in order to get the calcium your body needs.

Countin' Calcium

Food	Amount of Calcium
Low-fat milk (1 cup)	300 mg
Swiss cheese (1 ounce)	272 mg
Cheddar cheese (1 ounce)	204 mg
American cheese (1 ounce)	124 mg
Low-fat yogurt (1 cup)	400-450 mg
Ice cream (1 cup)	70 mg
Frozen yogurt (1 cup)	200-300 mg
Orange (1 medium)	56 mg
Broccoli (1/2 cup cooked)	36 mg
Beans (1/2 cup)	41 mg
Calcium-enriched orange juice (1 cup)	333 mg
Calcium-enriched bread (2 slices)	580 mg

Pump Up the Iron

No, we're not talking about lifting weights. We mean the mineral iron, which your body needs to keep your blood healthy. When girls get their period each month, their bodies lose iron along with blood. If you don't eat iron-rich foods to replace the lost iron, you may feel weak and tired. A low iron level in the blood is called iron-deficiency anemia. It is very common among girls because of monthly blood loss and a poor intake of iron in their diet.

Having anemia means that your blood has a reduced ability to carry oxygen to your body cells and tissues. This can result in feeling totally wiped out and being unable to do your normal amount of activity or exercise. Even worse, you could start experiencing headaches, dizziness, shortness of breath, and generally not feeling like your usual awesome self. It can also affect your schoolwork because if you're tired all the time, you'll be unable to stay sharp in class. What can you do to prevent anemia? Eat foods with more iron, of course! Include iron-rich foods at every meal. Vitamin C will help your body absorb the iron better, so try to have both in the same meal.

Pumped Up with Iron
Lean meats like steak, chicken, and turkey
Iron-fortified breakfast cereals
Raisins
Spinach
Apricots
Beans

Vitamin C Superstars
Oranges and orange juice
Grapefruit
Broccoli
Cantaloupe
Green and red peppers

Fat or Fiction?

4 What's the story on fat? Everybody is talking about fat these days, whether they are trying to lose weight or just stay healthy. We are bombarded with information about fat almost every day—on television, in the news, in magazines, and from well-meaning friends and family members. Good fat, bad fat, fat free, and reduced fat—they're all so confusing! How can you tell if you are getting too much? What's a girl to do?

Fat?

If you can't tell fat from fiction, don't despair. Here's a mini-lesson on the "fats of life."

The Fats of Life

Fat is an essential nutrient that everybody needs for good health—no lie! It also adds flavor to food. Unfortunately, most Americans eat too much fat. Fat has gotten a bad rap for two reasons: It is higher in calories than any other nutrient, and certain types of fat can contribute to heart disease. A fatty diet greatly increases the risks of heart disease and cancer. Too much fat will make you overweight and possibly obese, and obesity puts you at serious risk for a whole bunch of diseases.

You've probably also heard that cholesterol is bad news. Cholesterol is a substance found in our bodies and in animal products such as meat and dairy foods. Saturated fat and cholesterol in your food can raise your blood cholesterol level. A high blood cholesterol level is one of the risk factors for heart disease and stroke. You don't need to worry too much about cholesterol in your teen years, but making good food choices now can slow down or stop the buildup of fat and cholesterol in your arteries. Don't go overboard on avoiding fat, though. Following a fat-free diet is unhealthy. It's also nearly impossible to stick to—and just plain boring.

How Much Is Too Much?

It's easy to be confused about how much fat we need. So what's the real deal? Although we all need some fat, most of us get too much, especially the saturated kind. That doesn't mean that you have to give up chocolate, pizza, ice cream, or other goodies, however. How can we enjoy the foods we really like and still eat healthily? The idea is to eat higher-fat foods less often and to choose healthy, great-tasting foods such as fruit, veggies, and grains more frequently. You can still enjoy your favorite treats—just not every day. If you eat a lot of high-fat foods in one meal, plan to make lower-fat choices for the next. It's all about balance.

ow to Eat Less Fat

In addition to eating more fruits and veggies and switching to low-fat or nonfat milk, there are zillions of other ways to cut excess fat from your diet. Here are a few:

1. *Eat lean meats that are baked, broiled, boiled, or grilled instead of fried. Choosing lean cuts of meat such as skinless chicken or turkey and cutting down on fatty ones like regular sausage, deep-fried chicken, and giant burgers is an easy way to lower your fat intake.*

2. *Try lower-fat versions of some of your high-fat favorites. Choosing low-fat or nonfat frozen yogurt instead of ice cream or opting for low-fat salad dressing instead of the regular kind can trim fat from your diet in a hurry. The best news is that most low-fat versions of high-fat foods taste great, so you won't notice any difference. (Just because it's low-fat doesn't mean you can pig out, though!)*

3. *Add less fat to your food. Mayonnaise, butter, cheese, gravy, and salad dressing can each add a hefty amount of fat to a meal. Cut what you normally use in half, find a replacement (mustard instead of mayo, jam instead of butter, etc.), or try the low-fat version.*

Extra, Extra: The Scoop on Snacking

Snacking is bad for you, right? Wrong! Snacking is not necessarily a bad habit. It all depends on the kinds of snacks you choose. In fact, many health experts recommend fueling up on several mini-meals throughout the day instead of three big ones. Traveling down the road to healthier eating habits can be a challenge, but eating the right snacks can help you along the way. Healthy snacks can boost your energy level and help you get the well-balanced variety of foods you need each day.

So why do people say that snacking is bad for you? Well, it definitely is—if you often stuff yourself with fatty, sugary foods. You know what that means:

soda, chocolate, candy, chips, cookies, cake, doughnuts, and ice cream. When you fill up on these kinds of snacks, you leave little room for other foods. And even if you eat the foods you need along with these snacks, you will probably end up with too much fat and too many calories. These treats are okay once in a while, but snacks from one of the major food groups should be your first choice. Reading food labels can also help you make good snack decisions. Remember—you always have a choice, and usually you can make a good one if you take the time to compare options. You want to get the most bang for your buck, nutritionally speaking: a snack that is low in fat and high in nutrients.

Snacks You'll Want to "Chews"
Cereal with low-fat milk
Pretzels
Vanilla wafers
Raw veggies dunked in salsa or in low-fat salad dressing
Fresh fruit dunked in low-fat yogurt
Fruit-flavored low-fat yogurt
Light microwave popcorn
Canned fruit packed in its own juice
100 percent fruit juice
Low-fat or nonfat frozen yogurt
Pudding made with low-fat milk
Graham crackers or animal crackers
Banana with peanut butter
Low-fat granola bars

Does this mean farewell to chips and chocolate bars forever? Not a chance! It's not realistic to say that you are never going to eat another candy bar or bag of chips, nor should you have to. All foods can fit into a healthy diet. To improve your snacking habits, try some of the following ideas to help you balance the less nutritious snack choices with good ones:

> • Bring healthy snacks from home instead of using vending machines or stopping at the convenience store. Pack boxes of dried fruit (raisins, apricots, etc.) or low-fat granola bars.
> • Create a small "junk food" budget for yourself each week and pledge not to spend a penny more.
> • Find healthy foods you like as much as the high-cal, low-nutrition ones you are replacing.

Fast-Food Factoids

Did you know that the average person spends about $250 a year in fast-food restaurants? Wow. Think about what you could get with that money if you saved it instead. But since avoiding fast food as a way to save money is not always a realistic option for the average girl, you need to learn how to make healthy choices when dining out. Most people love fast food—it tastes good, and it's convenient and cheap.

It also gives us a place to socialize with our friends and just hang out. Fast-food restaurants surround us, and their owners target teens by opening their restaurants near schools and by using clever advertisements.

You don't have to give up eating fast food, but you can put some thought into what you are choosing. Many fast-food chains have responded to the need for healthier choices by offering a few menu items that are lower in fat. Some even post the nutritional content of their foods so you can compare the fat and calories in each item. Try to limit fast foods to once or twice a week, and eat smaller amounts when you do splurge. Don't feel that you always need to clean your plate!

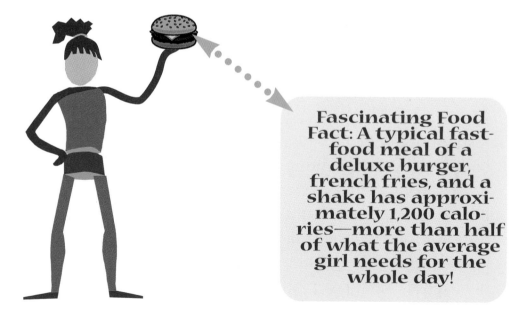

Fascinating Food Fact: A typical fast-food meal of a deluxe burger, french fries, and a shake has approximately 1,200 calories—more than half of what the average girl needs for the whole day!

Weighty Matters

According to experts, too little exercise is the greatest cause of people being overweight. What's the connection with food? Food supplies the energy you need to grow and be active. If you eat more than your body can burn, extra energy turns into fat.

Every day you get energy by taking in calories from food, and you use energy by—well, just by existing. (You even burn calories when you sleep, just not as many as when you are awake.) It is the balance of how many calories you eat with how

many your body burns that determines if you will gain, lose, or maintain your weight. So do you need to count calories every day? You don't have to if you are eating according to the food pyramid and getting regular exercise.

If you have gained a few pounds, it's probably just because you're growing and your body is changing. But if you're dead-set on losing some weight, the best and safest way is to increase your activity level while cutting back on "extras"—especially fatty ones—that you may not need. Most girls have a strong desire to fit in and look good, and American society often thinks looking good means being thin. This makes you a major target for the diet industry. But don't be fooled: Fasting or skipping meals, diet pills, and fad diets don't work and can be dangerous. What does work is staying positive; getting enough exercise; chowing on regular, healthy meals and snacks; and scarfing down fewer fatty foods. Doing all that may not make you as thin as a super-model (of course, in real life, who is?), but it will make you healthy. Healthy habits = a healthy attitude. If you have that, you won't obsess about your size.

You may want to ask your family doctor if you need to lose weight and have him or her refer you to someone who can help. Seeing a regis-tered dietitian—a health professional whose specialty is food and healthy eating—can be very useful. A dietitian can help you determine how and what you need to change in order to be successful at losing weight.

Exercise

So now you know why eating well is important, and you've got a good idea of how to do it. But eating well is not enough by itself to keep you fit and fabulous. You need regular activity to be your best.

If just the thought of exercise makes you shudder, chew on this: Exercise can help keep off extra weight, make you feel more energetic, reduce stress, tone muscles, improve your resistance to colds, and even help keep your skin looking healthy. Best of all, it's usually a lot of fun. Sounds too good to be true, doesn't it? Don't take our word for it; turn off the computer and the television and go, girl!

You don't have to sweat for hours to reap the benefits of exercise. Any type of activity—even walking or yard work—can improve your health and fitness. More vigorous activities like swimming, running, biking, and jumping rope will help condition your heart. The fact that exercise can also make you look better in your new jeans is just a bonus.

The key is making exercise a lifelong good habit, not just a temporary fix for a specific goal. For good health, experts recommend thirty to forty-five minutes a day of moderate activity like walking, cycling, dancing, jogging, swimming, or volleyball.

Getting with the Program

Getting started on the exercise habit is the hardest part. If you consider yourself a couch potato, don't expect to be out running the mile at warp speed within a week. Here are some tips to get you going:

Try to increase your activity by a small amount each week.
Take the stairs instead of the elevator.
Walk whenever you can.
Find activities you enjoy so you don't dread exercise.
Change your routine often to prevent boredom.
Try new activities—be adventurous.
Track your progress in a journal or on the computer.
Team up with a pal.

There are more exercise choices out there than you can even count, so if the first one or two you try don't thrill you, never fear—just keep trying, and you'll find the right type of activity for you.

The Master Plan

Eating regular meals and snacks through-out the day is important to meeting your body's needs. You couldn't possibly get all the nutrients you need from only one or two meals each day. This way of eating may lead to poor food choices and overeating because you get too hungry to think clearly. Irregular meals may be one of the reasons many girls are overweight. In fact, if you skip meals in an effort to lose weight, you may get so hungry that you end up eating whatever is in sight. Your body actually prefers smaller, more frequent meals to stay energized.

Breakfast Is Basic

You've heard it a million times, but that's just

7

because it's true: Breakfast really is the most important meal of the day. It fuels you up with enough energy to learn and be active. It can help you concentrate better in school and feel energized. Breakfast makes a difference in how you feel all day. Don't have time, you say? With a little planning, you can get the best possible start to your day. If you usually skip breakfast to catch a little extra snooze time, try going to bed a few minutes earlier so you'll be rested and still have time for a meal in the morning. Quick and easy breakfast ideas include granola bars, bagels, English muffins, cereal, and frozen waffles. Add a glass of milk and some juice or fruit, and you're on your way to a healthy day.

Fuel Up—A Sample Day of Eating Well

This is a sample day of eating the food pyramid way, with all of the recommended servings from each group included. If you use this sample meal plan as a guideline, you'll be fueled up and feelin' great full-time.

Breakfast
1 cup of cereal (grain group)
3/4 cup of orange juice (fruit group)
1 slice of wheat toast with jam (grain group/"extras" group)
1 cup of low-fat milk (milk group)

Lunch
2-3 slices of turkey (meat group)
2 slices of wheat bread (grain group)
1 teaspoon of low-fat mayonnaise ("extras" group)
Carrot and celery sticks (vegetable group)
Apple (fruit group)
1 cup of low-fat chocolate milk (milk group)

Snack
1 cup of low-fat fruit yogurt (milk group)
3 graham crackers (grain group)

Dinner
Grilled chicken breast (meat group)
Salad with low-fat salad dressing (vegetable group/"extras" group)
1 cup of rice (grain group)
1/2 cup of cooked broccoli (vegetable group)
3/4 cup of 100% fruit juice (fruit group)
1 slice of bread with margarine (grain group/"extras" group)

Snack
Light microwave popcorn (grain group)

Still having trouble figuring out how to change your eating habits to healthy ones? Take it slow—changing the way you eat for life is a big deal, and it won't happen overnight. But don't give up. The food pyramid, regular activity, common sense, and a positive attitude are all you need to pull it together for a healthy, happy you.

anemia   A condition that results from having too little iron in the blood.

bone mass   The total amount of bone in a person's body.

calcium   A substance found in certain foods that is stored in human bones and is necessary for proper bone development.

calorie   A unit of the energy found in food.

carbohydrates   One of the essential nutrients that we get from food.

fat   One of the essential nutrients that we get from food.

fiber   A substance in some foods that helps move food through the digestive system.

food pyramid   A guide for eating a variety of healthy foods in the right amounts each day.

iron   A substance found in certain foods that is necessary for healthy blood.

lactose intolerance   A condition that makes people unable to digest milk (and sometimes other dairy products) properly.

nutrient   Any substance or ingredient in food that gives us energy, helps us grow, or has other benefits for our bodies.

obese   Extremely overweight. Many experts consider a person obese if he or she weighs over 25 percent more than the recommended body weight.

osteoporosis   A condition in which bones become weak, brittle, and porous (full of holes or spaces).

protein   One of the essential nutrients that we get from food.

registered dietitian   A health care professional who specializes in meal planning and nutrition.

vegan   Someone who does not eat any food that comes from an animal.

vegetarian   Someone who does not eat meat but may eat eggs and dairy products.

It's a Girl's World:
helpful info

Web sites:

KidsHealth
http://www.kidshealth.org/teen/nutrition/index.html

Nutrition Cafe
http://www.exhibits.pacsci.org/nutrition

Nutrition Central
http://nutrition.central.vt.edu

Ten Tips to Eating Healthy and Physical Activity
http://ificinfo.health.org/brochure/10tipkid.htm

USDA Food Guide Pyramid
http://nal.usda.gov:8001/py/pmap.htm

To order a pamphlet on the U.S. Department of Agriculture's (USDA's) Food Guide Pyramid, contact:
Center for Nutrition Policy and Promotion
1120 20th Street NW
Suite 200, North Lobby
Washington, DC 20036

To learn more about other food pyramids, contact:
Oldways Preservation and Trust
25 First Street
Cambridge, MA 02141
Tel: (617) 621-3000
Fax: (617) 621-1230
e-mail: oldways@tiac.net
Web site: http://www.oldwayspt.org/html/pyramid.html

By the Book:
further reading

Bennett, Paul. *Healthy Eating.* Parsippany, NJ: Silver Burdett Press, 1997.

Galperin, Ann. *Nutrition.* Broomall, PA: Chelsea House, 1991.

Jukes, Mavis. *It's a Girl Thing: Nutrition.* New York: Alfred A. Knopf, 1999.

Klavan, Ellen. *The Vegetarian Factfinder.* New York: Little Bookroom, 1997.

Moss, Miriam. *Eat Well.* Parsippany, NJ: Silver Burdett Press, 1993.

Parker, Steve. *Professor Protein's Fitness, Health, Hygiene, and Relaxation Tonic.* Brookfield, CT: Millbrook Press, 1996.

Parsons, Alexandra. *I'm Happy, I'm Healthy!* Danbury, CT: Franklin Watts,1997.

Reef, Catherine. *Eat the Right Stuff.* New York: Twenty-First Century Books, 1995.

Zonderman, Jan, and Laurel Shader, MD. *Nutritional Diseases.* New York: Twenty-First Century Books, 1995.

Index

About the Author

Leslie Levchuck is a registered dietitian who works primarily with children and adolescents. She enjoys cooking, swimming, and staying fit. Ms. Levchuck lives in Long Island, New York, with her husband, Sean, and their son, Connor. This is her first book for young people.

Photo Credits

Cover photo, pp. 6, 8, 9, 17, 20, 24, 28, 32, 33, 37, 42 by Scott Bauer; p. 22, 23 © John Michael/International Stock; p. 29 by John Bentham

Series Design

Laura Murawski

Layout

Oliver Rosenberg